TATE GALLERY
Drawing
A young artist's guide

Jude Welton

TATE GALLERY CONSULTANT Colin Grigg

DORLING KINDERSLEY
LONDON • NEW YORK • STUTTGART

A DORLING KINDERSLEY BOOK

Project Art Editor Jacquie Gulliver
Project Editor Emma Johnson
U.S. Editor Camela Decaire
Editor Claire Watts
Designer Nicky Webb

Managing Editor Helen Parker
Managing Art Editor Peter Bailey
Picture Research Lorna Ainger
Production Louise Barratt

Photography Dave King

First American Edition 1994
Reprinted 1995
Published in the United States by
Dorling Kindersley Publishing, Inc., 95 Madison Avenue
New York, New York 10016

Distributed by Houghton Mifflin Company, Boston.

Library of Congress Cataloging-in-Publication Data
Welton, Jude.
 Drawing: a young artist's guide / by Jude Welton. –
1st American ed.
 p.   cm. – (The Young Artist)
 Includes index.
 ISBN 1-56458-676-6
 1. Drawing–Technique–Juvenile literature.
[1. Drawing–Technique.] I. Title. II. Series.
NC655.W43 1994
741.2–dc20   94–13103
                                                     CIP
                                                     AC

Color reproduction by Colourscan, Singapore
Printed and bound in Italy by L.E.G.O

Contents

Introduction to drawing

People have been drawing since the earliest times. And, since you were old enough to hold a crayon and make scribbles on a piece of paper, you have probably been drawing, too. Drawing is a language, and just as you tell other people what you see, think, and feel through writing and speaking, so you can through drawing. When you want to speak to a particular person, you choose exactly the right words and tone of voice. In the same way, when you draw, you need the right materials and techniques to express your ideas. In this book, you can see the ideas and techniques of other artists and find out how to use them in your own drawings. This can help you understand and enjoy art – and develop your own unique way of drawing.

Aboriginal rock drawing
This ancient drawing of kangaroos was found in New South Wales, Australia.

Early drawings

Prehistoric people drew on rocks with colored earth and plant dyes. Rock painters made use of the unevenness of rock surfaces, so a hole is often an eye, or a crack the line of a leg.

The real thing

No printed drawing can replace the experience of studying the real thing. The size of a drawing is an important part of its meaning, and in books, you cannot tell how big an image actually is. Drawings are best looked at up-close, where you can see the surface texture and identify how each mark was made. In printing, much of the detail is lost.

Zoom in
This is the size of Isabella's eye in the real drawing. Can you see some of the individual marks Rubens made?

Drawing with lines

Some drawings are detailed and take a long time to do, but others are done much more quickly. In this drawing, in the style of English cartoonist Phil May, the character of a child is shown with just a few lines. The drawing concentrates on the mouth and screwed-up nose and eyes – the features that express the most about a crying child. Always study your subject carefully and look for powerful features.

Drawing in the style of
PHIL MAY

SIR PETER PAUL RUBENS *Portrait of Isabella Brant 1622*

In this portrait of his first wife, Rubens used what was called the "three crayon technique," with black, white, and reddish chalks. Notice how detailed and naturalistic the face is, giving the woman an expression filled with curiosity. Can you see where and why Rubens has used each color?

Idea collection

Ideas can come from looking at the world around you – you can draw your house, your friends, family, pets, landscapes, or objects. Choose things that mean something to you, so that your drawings show something about you, too.

The pencil symbol

Where you see this symbol, you will find an idea or a subject to draw. Try the projects outlined in this book, but also use them as starting points for your own drawing experiments.

Your own drawings

In some parts of this book, you will be shown techniques to experiment with and develop. But feel free to express your own ideas and feelings when you draw, and don't think that you should be drawing like an adult. Picasso, one of the greatest artists of the 20th century, said that it took him a lifetime to learn to draw like a child!

LUCIEN (aged 9)
A Bird 1994

Wild imagination

Drawing is never just a matter of copying what you see. A drawing is a creation formed by marks on a surface, which tells us as much about the artist as it does about what he or she drew.

Ink blots
If you use your imagination, you can see pictures in abstract shapes like smudges and ink blots.

Learning from other artists

Looking at other people's drawings can teach you a great deal. Throughout this book, you will see examples of the work of artists from different times and cultures. Sometimes details have been pinpointed to help you explore the effects that have been created.

PABLO PICASSO *Head 1912*

In contrast to the drawing by Rubens on the opposite page, Picasso's dark, powerful charcoal drawing shows a head with features so distorted that it looks like an alien spaceman! When he drew this, Picasso was interested in African masks, and he tried to express some of their feeling in his work.

Techniques

Throughout the book you will find instructions to help you learn the techniques of drawing, from using a grid to enlarge your work, to learning how to draw people as they move. Don't worry if your drawings don't look like the photographs. They are just guidelines to help you.

Instructions
Step-by-step photographs and instructions will give you practical advice to help you learn new techniques.

Keeping your drawings

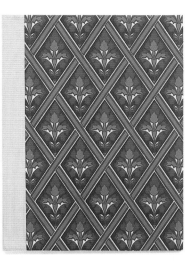

You probably won't have room to display all your drawings at once, so you will need somewhere to keep them safe. If you store your work carefully, the pictures will not become torn or faded. You can keep pages loose inside a portfolio or make a sturdy book to stick them in. A cardboard box of the right size and shape can be used, too. The best way to protect a really large drawing is to roll it up loosely. Use rubber bands to keep it rolled up, or buy a large cardboard tube to put it in.

Scrapbook

Take care
When you are drawing with soft materials, such as pastels, conté crayons, and charcoal, be careful not to smudge your work.

No smudges
You can seal materials that smudge easily with a spray fixative. Lay newspaper on the floor and place your drawing on top. Spray a light coat of fixative all over the surface. Leave it to dry, then add another fine coat.

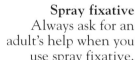

Spray fixative
Always ask for an adult's help when you use spray fixative.

Smudging effects
If you want to smudge a charcoal drawing on purpose, you can use a kneaded eraser.

Keeping clean
When you are drawing with charcoal, put a piece of clean paper over the part of the drawing you are not working on, so that you don't accidentally smudge it.

LÉON BONVIN *Interior with Still Life c.1856*

This charcoal drawing was done before spray fixative was invented. Bonvin used a varnish called "shellac," which he diluted with alcohol and sprayed on through a mouth-tube to seal his work.

Tissue paper
You can protect a favorite drawing by making a tissue paper cover. Cut a sheet of tissue paper the same width as your drawing but slightly longer. Line up the paper with the bottom of the drawing and fold the overlapping piece over the picture at the top. Glue or tape this flap to the back.

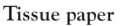

Unsmudged charcoal line

Smudged charcoal line

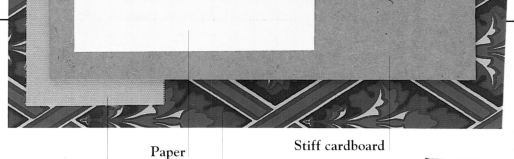

Strong fabric   Paper   Stiff cardboard

Wallpaper or wrapping paper

Strong thread

Darning needle

Ruler

Fabric tape

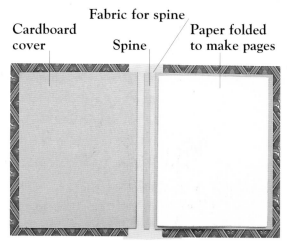

Cardboard cover   Fabric for spine   Paper folded to make pages

Spine

A book for your drawings

It is useful to have a strong book both for keeping your drawings in and for sketching. If you make your own, it can be any size you want: a huge one for your large drawings, or a tiny one to keep in your pocket. You can choose different papers for your pages, too, depending on what you want to use them for. (Turn to pages 38-39 for lots of ideas on how to use your book.) You should find everything you need in an arts and crafts store, but you may want an adult's help to make your book.

1 Cut two equal pieces of cardboard for the covers. Then, cut two pieces of wallpaper slightly larger than the covers. Cut a thin strip of cardboard for the spine and a strip of strong fabric to cover it. Cut and fold sheets of paper in half to make pages. Trim the edges so that the pages are just smaller than the covers.

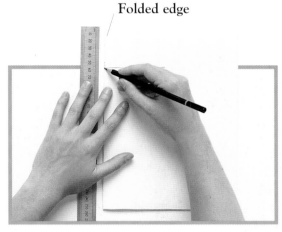

Folded edge

2 Measure the width of the fabric tape. Then, divide the length of the pages into five rough sections. At each section, mark the width of the fabric tape on the folded edge of the paper.

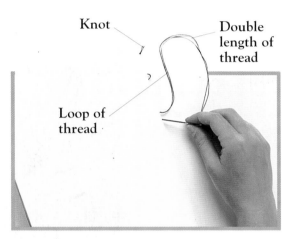

Knot   Double length of thread

Loop of thread

3 Push the threaded needle through near the top of the fold. Push it out near the first mark, then in at the second, leaving a loop. Repeat at each mark. At the bottom, cut off, but don't tie, the thread.

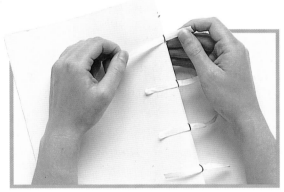

4 Cut four equal lengths of fabric tape. Slip each one through one of the loops of thread, with the sticky side away from the paper. Pull the thread tight and tie the end.

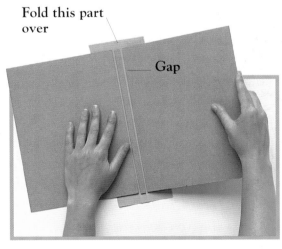

Fold this part over

Gap

5 Put glue on the strip of fabric, then place the cardboard spine in the center of it. Lay the covers on either side of the spine, leaving a small gap. Fold the fabric over at the top and bottom.

6 Place the pages on the covers and stick the tape to the cardboard. Glue the wallpaper to the outside of each cover. Glue a second strip of fabric over the binding. Fold the edges over neatly.

Weigh it down
Close the finished book and place some heavy objects on it. Leave it for about a week, until the glue is dry.

7 Cut two sheets of paper slightly smaller than the covers. Glue the sheets to the inside, over the seams and tape.

Drawing tools

Y ou don't have to limit drawing to pencil and white paper. Look at how the artists in this book have selected the materials and way of working most suited to the intention of their drawings. Take time to decide what surface, tools, and technique you need for your purpose. Each drawing tool, whether it is an oil pastel or a feather dipped in ink, is like a musical instrument, with its own particular range and character.

Fine felt tip

Fat felt tip

Brush felt tip

Serrated felt tip

Soft pastels

Large soft pastels

Graphite pencil

Thick charcoal

Medium charcoal

Fine charcoal

Soft pastels crumble easily, so always handle them with care. The easiest way to buy a range of colors is in a boxed set.

Medium HB lead pencil

Soft 6B lead pencil

Cotton swabs

Pencil eraser

Sketching pencil

Pencil sharpener
When you need a thin, precise line, you should keep your pencils sharp. At other times, when you need a soft, fuzzy tone, it is best to use a blunter pencil.

Kneaded eraser for rubbing out soft pencil, charcoal, and pastel.

A soft tone
You can get a softer tone by rubbing your charcoal drawing with a cotton swab, or you can use it to blend tones.

Water-soluble pencils

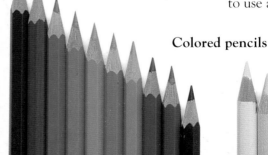

Colored pencils

Pencils are given letters and numbers that tell you how hard or soft they are, and how dense. For example, a 6H pencil is hard and light, while a 6B is soft and dark, with HB falling in the middle. Colored pencils are not graded; they are sold by color.

Wax crayons

Toothpicks for drawing on a wax surface (page 24).

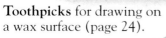

Blue ink   Yellow ink   Red ink   Black ink

Drawing pen

Balsa wood can be used for drawing with inks. Cut it to the size you want.

Pen and ink has been used for drawing for centuries. A quill pen made from goose feathers was the most common drawing tool in the past, although reeds and bamboo were also used.

Brown package paper (matte side)

Oil pastels are stickier than soft pastels because they contain oil. The colors blend well, too.

Pastel or charcoal paper

Acid-free pastel or charcoal paper

HENRY MOORE *Pink and Green Sleepers 1941*

During World War II, many people in London took shelter from enemy bombers underground in the subway. Henry Moore sketched these two restless sleepers in the dark tunnels. He drew in wax crayon, later brushing over it with watercolor. Because wax is water-resistant, the drawing shows through. Can you see how this technique captures the drama of the situation and shows the form of the figures rather than just their outline?

White cartridge paper

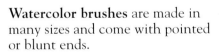

Conté crayons are a hard version of chalk and come in many colors.

Watercolor paper

Paper is available in all sorts of colors, textures, and weights. Drawing materials produce different effects on different papers.

Watercolor brushes are made in many sizes and come with pointed or blunt ends.

Watercolors come in cake form in small, square tins, and in liquid form in tubes.

Pastel paper

Watercolor palette for mixing paints and diluting inks

Sponge for washes

Sketchpad

Lines and marks

Line is the basic language of drawing, from a baby's first scribble to an inventor's plans. You can draw lines in all sorts of ways. If the tool you use has a flexible point, such as a fine brush, then you can change the quality of a line by varying the pressure as you draw. Whether you use long, flowing lines or short, broken ones will affect the character and meaning of the drawing. Jagged lines can create a sense of unease, for example, while smooth, flowing lines feel calm and peaceful. Think about the quality you want your drawing to have and try to use lines that express it.

Conté crayon

Pencil

Pen

Flamelike trees
In van Gogh's drawing below, the cypress trees are drawn with heavy, black, parallel pen strokes. They seem to flicker like dark flames in the landscape.

Curves
Van Gogh used closely spaced, curving lines, which flow across the picture like waves, for the distant mountains.

Dots
Black and gray dots mark the tips of the wheat sheaves.

Wavy lines
Billowing clouds are drawn with fine, wavy lines that suggest movement.

VINCENT VAN GOGH *Wheatfield with Cypresses* 1889

The Dutch artist van Gogh believed nature was filled with spiritual forces. This drawing shows a field of corn blown by the wind, with clouds swirling overhead. Each living thing in the drawing is given its own pattern of marks, creating a sense of rhythm and sweeping movement across the landscape.

 Using lines
Experiment with using different sorts of lines to draw the same image. See how this changes the meaning.

Dotted lines
In the first drawing, the line is broken up with dots, which makes the hare appear fluffy and gentle.
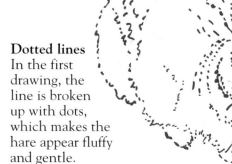

Dashes
In this drawing, a mixture of lines and dashes is used. What quality do you think the hare has here?

Continuous line
Heavy, even pressure creates a continuous flowing line that makes the hare look fiercer than in the other drawings.

Fine charcoal   Medium charcoal   Graphite pencil

Lines and feelings

Try this exercise to see how lines can express feelings. You can make an abstract drawing or a portrait or scene. Use different drawing tools as well as colored papers.

Choose a paper color:

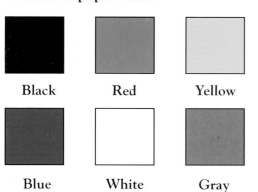

Black   Red   Yellow

Blue   White   Gray

Choose a feeling to draw:

Anger   Irritation
Happiness   Fear
Sadness   Calm
Loneliness   Boredom
Humor   Friendliness
Tiredness   Confidence

ERNST LUDWIG KIRCHNER *Berlin Street Scene 1913*

The German artist Kirchner was an Expressionist painter who exaggerated line to express feeling. City life fascinated him and he drew many street scenes. In this pastel drawing, he used harsh color with strong, dark lines to express the aggressive atmosphere of a crowded street.

Flick of the wrist
A zigzag is all that is needed to show the white feathers in the middle woman's hat.

Expressive line
Kirchner crossed the lines to make his drawing more expressive. He used thick, jagged lines for the background figures.

Busy lines
Light scribbles add to the feeling of busy movement.

Footwork
Taken on their own, these black lines are difficult to recognize as a leg and foot.

Below you can see two drawings that children made to express their feelings.

GARRY (aged 10) *Anger 1994*
Black and blue crayon on white paper

ROSEMARY (aged 11)
Sadness 1994
Pencil on yellow paper

Drawing with confidence

On a large piece of paper, draw bold, flowing lines, moving your whole arm, not just your hand. Draw freely and confidently, then compare the result to a drawing in which you have used more controlled hand movements. What differences do you see?

15

Light and shade

The way light falls on an object tells us about its form and texture. Have you noticed the contrast between light and shade on sunny days, and the duller tones on cloudy days? Drawing usually involves making dark marks on lighter paper; that is, we draw the shade, not the light. This is called "chiaroscuro," which is Italian for "bright-dark." When you are drawing, make a note of where the light is coming from, and study the highlights, the darkest shades, and those in between. Use your observations to make flat images appear three-dimensional.

LEONARDO DA VINCI *Madonna of the Rocks c.1483*

Silverpoint is one of the oldest tools for drawing. A piece of pure silver is dragged across the surface of a specially coated paper, leaving a fine trace of silver that darkens with time. The lines it produces are very fine, almost ghostly. The Madonna's face is shaded using hundreds of fine parallel lines, while the cheek catching the light is a single dissolving line. Can you see the similarity between Leonardo's treatment of the oval face and the light falling on the egg?

Tonal scales

The lightness or darkness of a color, such as the shades of gray in the gradual change from black to white, is called "tone." There are many ways of showing variations in tone. Practice some of the techniques shown below.

Smooth as an egg

If you look at an egg, you can see that it has a smooth, curved surface because the shadow changes gradually from dark to light.

To create a lighter tone with wax crayon, gradually apply less pressure as you rub.

Dilute ink with water to lighten the tone.

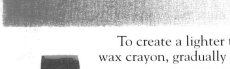

Add white to conté crayon to lighten the tone

Blend charcoal with a cotton swab until it fades to pale gray.

JOHN CONSTABLE
Fir Trees at Hampstead 1820

Notice how the pale trunks of the trees stand out against the dark leaves. The sunlight seems to come from the left.

Creating texture

Different methods of shading can suggest different textures. Experiment with marks and tones, using a selection of drawing tools, to get a variety of texture and form.

Dots

Drawing with dots is known as "stippling." You can alter the tone by varying the size of the dots and the space between them.

Zigzags

You can create shading by scribbling. Vary the pressure and closeness of the lines.

FRANCIS UNWIN *Cromer Hotels 1920*

Artists also use shade to create mood, and to direct the viewer's attention. In this seaside scene, Francis Unwin used light and shade not only to draw the forms of the buildings, but also to convey the feeling of a stormy day. As you look at the picture, you can imagine that thunder is rumbling in the background and that lightning could strike at any moment.

Hatching and cross-hatching
Unwin created darker tones by shading with a series of roughly parallel strokes, a technique called "hatching." In places, he crossed the lines with another layer at a different angle. This is called "cross-hatching." Can you see the hatching in Leonardo's drawing, too?

Simple forms

Always remember to observe where the light is coming from and how the light and shade show the form of an object. Experiment with simple shapes, using these observations. Use black or a dark color for the shadow, white for the highlighted area, and two tones in between for the shading. Your picture should start to appear three-dimensional.

Straight sides
In these shapes, the variation in shade is much easier to see. Each side is a different shade.

Shadows
Remember to look at the shadows, too. Each shape casts a different shadow.

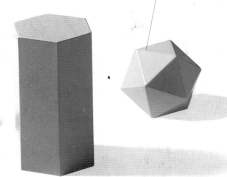

Curved sides
Here, the shade grows gradually.

Using color

Drawing need not be in black and white. You can draw in color with crayons or inks, or experiment with colored paper. Remember, you don't have to match the colors you see. Color can be used in drawings, just as it can in paintings, to create a mood or produce a decorative effect. Bright, contrasting colors will create a completely different feel from a drawing that is done in soft, similar, or harmonizing colors.

Primary colors

Red, blue, and yellow are called the "primary" colors. All the other colors can be made by mixing these three together in different amounts.

Secondary colors

By mixing two primaries together, you can make "secondary" colors.

Blue and yellow make green

Red and blue make purple

Complementary colors

Red and green, blue and orange, and yellow and purple are called "complementary colors." They are the colors that contrast the most when they are placed next to each other – making each appear at its brightest.

HANS HOFMANN *Color Intervals at Provincetown 1943*

German-born artist Hans Hofmann explored the way that certain colors seem to move away from you while others come toward you, which he called the "push and pull" of colors. In this drawing of a seaside town, he used ink lines to draw shapes, and roughly filled in between the lines with color. The colors have nothing to do with reality, but rather they create abstract patterns and effects.

Color impact

Hofmann has used sets of complementary colors in his drawing to give the picture impact and brightness. Can you spot them?

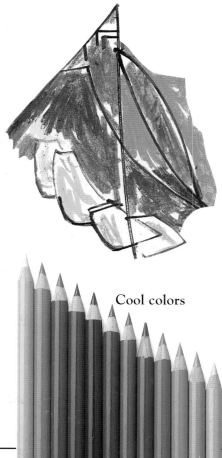

Cool colors

Light and color
The pale pink and flecks of green in the chandelier contrast with the bright colors of Lydia's dress and hair. Look at the way white light from the chandelier throws highlights onto Lydia's bare shoulder.

Bright contrast
Lydia's lemon yellow dress stands out against the purple shadow of the chair cushion behind her. These colors are complementary and so both look bright.

Colored papers
Another way of introducing color to your drawing is by using colored background paper.

Flesh tones
Rather than simply using a shade of pink, Cassatt built up the color using light crisscross lines of blue, yellow, and pink. The colors seem to blend together to form the tone and texture of Lydia's skin.

MARY CASSATT *At the Theater (Woman in a Loge) c.1879*

Mary Cassatt was an American artist who lived in Paris in the late 19th century. This lively pastel drawing shows her sister Lydia at the opera. You can imagine the artist hidden in the corner of the opera box, sketching her sister in her glamorous yellow evening dress. The bold colors are built up with quick pencil strokes. By leaving the strokes unblended, the paper texture and the colors underneath show through.

Creating mood

Colors with red in them – scarlet, orange, and golden-yellow, for example – are called "warm." They make us think of fire and sunshine. Colors with a lot of blue are called "cool." They remind us of water, ice, and plants. Warm and cool colors affect the mood of your picture. They also create a sense of depth, because warm colors appear to move toward you, while cool colors move away.

Warm colors

1 Using colored crayons or pastels, draw two versions of the same picture. For the first picture, use only cool blues and greens.

2 Use warm colors such as orange, purple, red, and yellow for the other drawing. What strikes you about the different moods of the two pictures?

Outline and shape

Artists use outline, or contour line, to show the edge of an object or where one object separates from another. Place a pair of scissors on paper and trace around them. If the line is of even thickness, the image you draw will look flat. You can make the scissors appear rounded or three-dimensional by varying the thickness of the line or using shading. Artists often use flat outlines and shapes to create decorative designs. Sometimes it's fun to concentrate on the shape of the objects you draw, rather than their solid forms.

Making shapes
Choose objects to draw and cut out that have very definite and contrasting shapes, with plenty of curves and angles.

Linking shapes
Overlap the shapes you have cut out to make other interesting shapes.

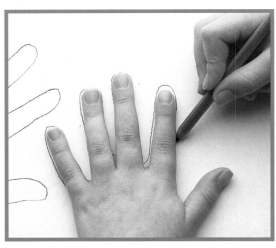

A simple outline
Draw around your hand. First use a thin, then a very thick line. See how different in character they are.

Cut-out pictures
Draw the outlines of several different objects. Use colored paper, or color in the shapes as you wish.

FERNAND LÉGER *The Birthday* 1950

The French artist Léger used a strong black outline to give his figures the qualities of a statue or monument. He was not interested in getting a photographic likeness, but wanted to create bold decorative designs of ordinary people.

Cut or tear out the shapes and glue them onto another sheet of paper to make your picture. You can overlap the shapes to create new forms or keep them separate.

Making silhouettes

Have you ever cast shadows on the wall with your fingers? You can create shadow shapes or silhouettes by setting an object between a light source and a sheet of paper or material. Experiment with drawing silhouettes. As well as drawing hand or foot silhouettes, try drawing the silhouette of a whole body. Attach a large sheet of paper to the wall and get a friend to stand next to it. You could play an identification game, too: try to recognize people by their silhouettes alone.

1 Ask your friend to stand very still while you trace around his or her shadow on white paper.

Black and white shapes

It is by recognizing shapes that we make sense of objects in our visual world. When we look in the distance, we often recognize someone we know by their shape, before we can make out the details of their appearance. Everything you see is made up of different shapes. Look carefully and you will spot them.

Distorted face
In these two drawings, the same black shapes are used, but in the first one, the white shapes in between are not in the right place, so the face looks distorted.

Composed face
In this drawing, the black shapes are carefully put together so that the white shapes in between form the features of the man's face.

2 Fill in the silhouette with black paint or crayon and cut it out. Try making silhouette portraits of family and friends by drawing their profiles (side view) on black cardboard and cutting them out.

Animal silhouette
Draw a simple animal outline and fill it in with ink or watercolor.

BRIAN GRIMWOOD *The Rickshaw 1994*

Illustrator Brian Grimwood has drawn many silhouettes using pen and ink and watercolor. Here he has used a brush to suggest the shapes of a Chinese rickshaw. Notice how the simple shapes, such as the man's legs and the wheel of the rickshaw, give some sense of the blur of movement as the vehicle is pulled along.

Pattern and texture

SHAHA (aged 10)
Winter 1993

You can find patterns all around you, in both natural objects, such as feathers, leaves, and shells, and manufactured objects, like fabrics, tiles, and carpets. Even your own skin has a pattern if you look closely. Sometimes a pattern is made up of lines only, and sometimes it is made up of different colored shapes. Every object has its own texture, too, which you can see as well as touch. Think about the way patterns and textures combine on the surface of objects, and how you can use these combinations in your drawings. Experiment with patterns that are just decorative, or make drawings that use patterns in a lifelike picture.

Natural pattern
The brilliant patterns on the skin of this poisonous lizard warn other animals to keep away. Natural markings – on leaves, insects, fish, and other creatures – can provide inspiration for your drawings.

MAURITS CORNEILLE ESCHER *Reptiles 1943*

The Dutch artist Escher was fascinated by optical illusions. In this drawing, he played with the idea of a flat pattern of reptiles coming to life, crawling off the page and around the desk, blending into the flat pattern again. Notice how the simple white, mid-gray, and dark gray reptile shapes fit together like a jigsaw puzzle.

Revealing a pattern
Find a leaf with a strong vein pattern. You can make a copy of it by taking a rubbing.

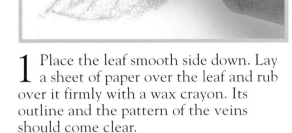

1 Place the leaf smooth side down. Lay a sheet of paper over the leaf and rub over it firmly with a wax crayon. Its outline and the pattern of the veins should come clear.

2 Use different colored crayons to make leaf rubbings all over the paper. Go over the lines with colored pencil to strengthen the pattern.

3 You can brush a thin coat of watercolor over your repeat design. The wax crayon will hold off the watercolor so that the full leaf pattern stands out against the background.

Natural and made
Look for patterns that appear both in nature and in manufactured objects such as fabric.

Sparkling color
The clear colors of beads and gemstones can inspire bright patterns.

Look closely
Collect shells and pebbles and look at their patterns through a magnifying glass.

SONIA BOYCE *Big Woman's Talk 1984*

In this seemingly simple portrait of a mother and daughter, British artist Sonia Boyce has added an element of tension by cropping off the mother's arms, legs, and head, leaving the viewer focused on the many bold and colorful patterns. The artist has filled in the areas between the ink outlines with flat areas of pastel color, treating the figures themselves in much the same way as the patterned fabric and wallpaper.

Drawing patterns
Make drawings of patterns that occur in nature. Look closely, perhaps with a magnifying glass, to help you discover patterns you might not spot at first. Shells and other objects on a beach have interesting patterns.

LEILA (aged 11)
Shell Pattern 1994

Draw a spiral
This fossil has a natural spiral pattern. Look at it for a while, close the book, and try to draw it.

Scratching and tracing

There are many other ways of drawing besides making black or colored marks on paper. You can create your own surfaces, with exciting textures and colors, or use unusual materials to draw with. Experiment and explore different techniques for drawing. Try those shown here, or invent a new method.

ZDENKA KABÁTOVÁ-TÁBORSKÁ *The Heron and the Crab 1992*

This looks like an old-fashioned woodblock print. In fact, it was done on scratchboard, black-surfaced cardboard with an underlayer of white, then photocopied and colored.

Color scratch drawings

Scratching out is an exciting way of drawing that has been used by many artists. Its proper name is "sgraffito," which is Italian for "scratched."

Colored wax crayons

Toothpick

1 First, cover your surface with patches of pale and brightly colored wax crayon.

2 Go over this with a thick coating of black wax crayon.

3 Draw your picture through the waxy surface, using a sharp tool such as a toothpick.

✏️ Transfer drawing

Paul Klee used this simple technique to make copies or slight variations of many of his drawings. With this process, he produced thousands of drawings in watercolor. Try it yourself with one of your drawings. All you need is a piece of linoleum, a roller, black oil paint, cardboard, watercolors, paper – and, of course, your original drawing.

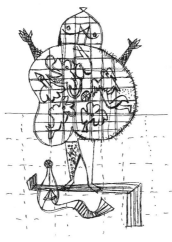

Original drawing based on a work by Paul Klee

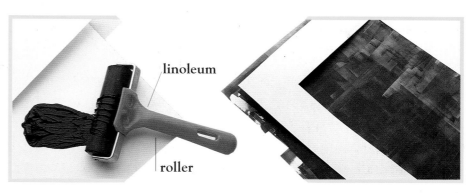

linoleum

roller

1 Put one or two blobs of black oil paint on the linoleum, then use the roller to flatten the paint evenly over the surface until you have a very thin layer.

2 Cut a square frame and place it over the painted surface. Place a blank sheet of paper over it.

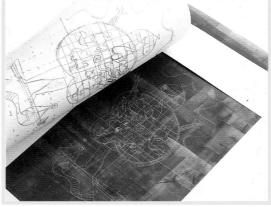

3 Place your drawing on top with the image facing you. Use a pencil to trace the edges of your drawing, pressing firmly, but not piercing the paper. Peel off the paper.

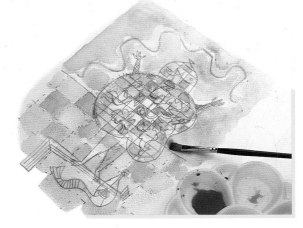

4 Let the oil-paint dry, then add watercolor touches to your transfer drawing. The outline of oil paint will stay sharp.

PAUL KLEE *They're Biting 1920*

Paul Klee was a Swiss watercolorist, painter, and etcher of fantastic and often humorous works. For this fanciful composition of someone fishing, Klee used the transfer technique shown on this page, which he called "Olfarbzeichnungen," German for "oil color drawing."

Finished transfer drawing

Drawing with a brush

Drawing with a brush, using inks or watercolors, is one of the most exciting ways of working. There is a long tradition of bold brush drawing in China and Japan, for every kind of subject. In these countries, brush drawing is closely linked to the flowing marks used for writing. You may think that if you use a brush, you are painting rather than drawing. There are no real rules, but if your picture is made up mainly of lines and marks, then you can describe it as a drawing. When you work with a brush, keep the lines simple and experiment with the effects of using one color or several.

Making a wash

Use watercolors (above) or inks to create completely different tones from other drawing materials. To make a wash, mix the ink or watercolor with water in a dish until it is thin. Use a large brush or a sponge to apply it.

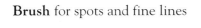

Brush for spots and fine lines

Flat brush for straight, flat lines

Medium brush for general use

Thick brushes for general use

Brush marks

Before you try doing a brush drawing, practice making marks like the ones shown here, and experiment with your own marks and lines. Use the tip of the brush to make a point, then press down gently to make a fatter line, and lift off toward the tip again to form a pointed end. Don't worry if your lines don't flow at first. Enjoy yourself, without being too concerned about the end result.

Oriental brush marks for flowers

Inks for use with brushes

Brush marks for grass

Oriental brushes

Fine brush

Medium brush

Broad brush

Brush marks for reeds

Oriental marks

These brush marks of plants and water are part of a traditional visual "vocabulary" of Chinese and Japanese brush marks.

Brush marks for water

 Ink applied with a broad brush

 **Ink** applied with a medium brush

  **Ink** applied undiluted

Ink thickened with poster paint

NAGASAWA ROSETSU
Shoki the Demon-queller Toad c.1787

With a few rapid brushstrokes, Japanese artist Rosetsu could create vivid pictures of people and animals. Notice how he has used simple, dark lines to draw the big, round eyes and drooping mouth.

Working with a brush

Find out what different effects you can get by using a wet and a dry brush, or different amounts of water to dilute your inks and watercolors. To work with a dry brush, dip your brush into the ink or paint and blot it with a piece of absorbent paper or rag, keeping just enough moisture on the brush to allow you to make marks.

Finding a subject
Practice drawing different shapes with watercolor paints. Simple forms suit watercolor well.

Flowing flowers

When you are more confident about using a brush, choose a subject that suits flowing lines, such as a vase of tulips with wavy stems. Using ink or paint, try working with a single color, then choose colors that match your subject. Look for the basic lines, and avoid fussy detail. Try using white paper, and dilute your ink or watercolor so that the whiteness shines through.

RAOUL DUFY *Open Window at Saint Jeannet 1926*

Dufy used a fluid brush laden with vivid colors to capture this sunny day in the south of France. He used a wash to suggest the shape of the window frame, then added lines to give it more definition. Compare this picture with van Gogh's wheat field (page 14). Which do you think is more alive?

1 Keep the brush wet and well loaded to help your lines flow freely. Wash the brush between colors.

2 You don't have to wait for one color to dry completely before you add the next – you can let colors run into each other.

Flowing colors
Notice the effect of letting colors run into each other.

3 Leave the drawing loose, rather than adding too much detail.

Composition and viewpoint

When you decide how to arrange the elements of a drawing on the page, you are composing your picture. A composition can be balanced or unbalanced, symmetrical (evenly proportioned) or asymmetrical (unevenly proportioned), depending on the effect the artist wants. Once you have chosen a subject, the viewpoint you choose is very important. It affects what is included, what is left out, the angle from which you show things, and how all the different elements relate to each other in terms of size, shape, and color. All these things give your drawing its own particular character. Whether you are working indoors or outside, drawing a still life, people, or a distant landscape, consider your subject from several different angles before starting.

Composing a still life

When you begin to compose a still life you need to think about two different things. First of all, you need to arrange the objects themselves. Then, decide on the viewpoint you are going to use for your drawing.

Near and far
Move the objects around to create different shapes and spaces.

Standing out

Compare these two still life drawings (above and below). By arranging the objects in various ways, you can focus on different objects and shapes, making one thing appear more important than another.

Cropping your picture

You don't have to draw the whole arrangement. You can select a part that interests you, or you can crop out part of the object and place it at a different angle. Look at the shapes made when objects overlap, and look at shapes between shapes.

GIORGIO MORANDI *Still Life 1933*

The Italian artist Morandi collected jugs, bottles, jars, and bowls, composing them in a variety of arrangements for his drawings, prints, and paintings. In this etching – a process in which the etcher draws on to a copper plate with a special needle – Morandi has crowded the objects into a dark forest of upright forms. These are separated in space by a range of finely cross-hatched tones. Notice how the white vase in the middle acts as a focus for the whole composition.

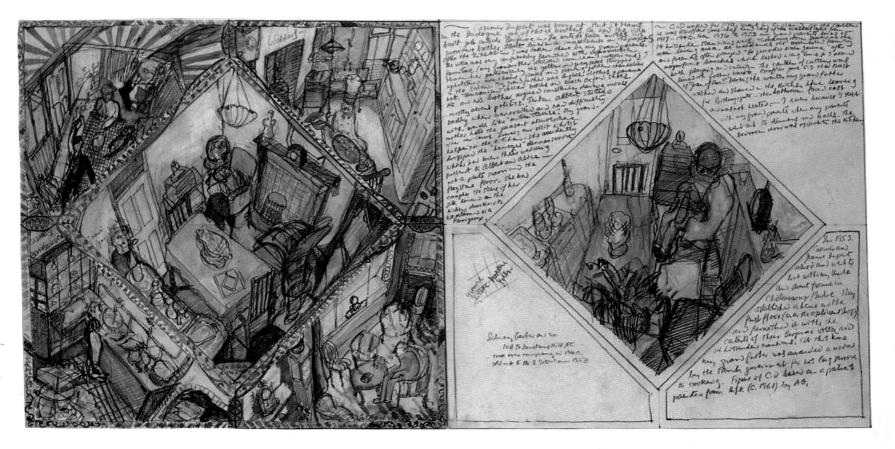

ANTHONY GREEN *Working drawing for "Casimir Dupont" 1980*

Anthony Green used these unusual shapes to illustrate the story of his French grandfather, Casimir Dupont. Around the central square of the drawing, there are scenes from Casimir Dupont's life. It is not easy to draw from such a high viewpoint, but you might get some idea of how to do this by taking the roof off a doll's house and looking in from above.

Portrait or landscape?

You can use your viewfinder to make your picture any shape you like. The most common shape for a picture is a rectangle. This can be either upright, which is known as "portrait" shape, or horizontal, which is called "landscape" shape.

A different picture

You can change the way a photograph or drawing looks by laying a viewfinder over it. Explore what happens when you hide bits of the picture, such as the sky or the top of someone's head. Make your own viewfinder with two L-shaped pieces of cardboard.

Landscape shape

Using a viewfinder

Holding the pieces of L-shaped cardboard together like a picture frame, use them to help you select the angle and the section of the subject that you want to include. There are ready-made viewfinders, too. You could use a doorway or a window to frame your picture.

L-shaped pieces of cardboard

Portrait shape

Near and far

Although you draw on a flat surface, real objects are not all flat, and they are certainly not all the same distance away from you. People and objects exist in three-dimensional space, which means that they have length, breadth, and depth. Some artists use a system called "perspective" in their work to imitate the way we see the real world, making objects appear nearer or farther away. You have probably noticed that things look smaller and less detailed the farther away from you they are. This simple principle is the basis for creating an illusion of space in a flat work of art.

Vanishing point

Perspective
Look at the way the figures get smaller as they get farther away. See, too, how the lines of the floor get closer together as they recede.

Vanishing point
The straight lines in the drawing lead the eye to a dot in the far distance. This dot, the point where the lines meet, is called the "vanishing point." It lies on the horizon line, which is at the artist's eye level.

Background
The buildings in the background are not much bigger than the boot of the man in the foreground.

Middle ground
The line of the bank on which the man is standing separates the foreground from the middle ground. The line of the buildings' roofs leads your eye toward the background.

Foreground
Look at how much detail there is in the face and clothes of the man in the foreground, and compare it to the tiny figure in the distant boat.

✎ Foreground to background
When you look at any scene, the area closest to you is called the foreground. The area farthest away is the background, and the area in between the two is the middle ground. Make a drawing in which the foreground, middle ground and background are clearly separated. Use the drawing by Ingres on the right to help you.

JEAN AUGUSTE DOMINIQUE INGRES *Portrait of Charles François Mallet 1809*

While he was living in Rome, the French artist Ingres drew this detailed portrait of a civil engineer named Mallet standing on the banks of the Tiber River. There is a strong diagonal line of perspective in the background, and the smallest buildings are lighter in tone than the tall figure in the foreground, accenting their distance from the viewer.

L. BIEDERMANN *The City of the Future 1916*

The secret of drawing imaginary places is to make them appear realistic. Drawn for a science fiction magazine many years ago, this city still seems futuristic today. Biedermann skillfully used perspective to suggest great size and vast distances as if we were looking down from a spaceship. Where do you think we are observing the scene from?

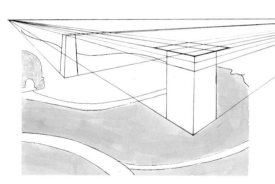

Up above
The artist has used a two-point perspective in the drawing above. That means that two vanishing points determine the position and angle of the buildings.

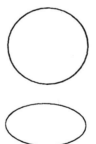

Changing circles
Viewing the city from high up, circular forms appear as squashed oval shapes or "ellipses." Can you see this effect when you look at the roads and rail tracks in the picture?

Foreshortening

This figure measures four squares as he lies on the floor. Viewed from the side (below), we can see that the squares are of equal size. But viewed from the end (right), the squares appear to be squashed, or "foreshortened," as they get farther away. If someone sits or lies in front of you, the part of their body closest to you can appear to be larger because of the perspective illusion of foreshortening.

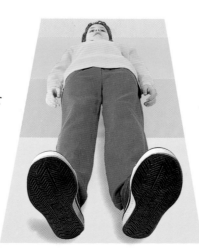

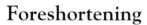

Big feet
Try drawing a foreshortened figure. Get a friend to lie on a table with their feet toward you and sit so that he or she is at eye level. You'll find that your friend's feet look huge, while the rest of the body looks squashed. Don't worry if your drawing looks odd – foreshortened figures do look strange!

Figures and faces

Y ou probably enjoy drawing real people or storybook characters from memory and imagination. It's also fun to work from life, using a model. Draw your family and friends, in groups and individually – and don't forget to make self-portraits. As always, looking is very important. Look at parts of the face and body in relation to each other, noting size and position. Try drawing feet, hands, and eyes. As well as making faces and figures lifelike and accurate, try to capture character and expression in your work.

EDGAR DEGAS *Three Studies of a Dancer in Fourth Position 1879–80*

The French artist Edgar Degas made these studies of a 14-year-old dancer for a sculpture. You can imagine the artist walking around the young ballerina, drawing her from three main viewpoints. Notice that he didn't get the leg positions quite right in the right-hand study, and changed the drawing as he worked.

Ready to bat
As the top of the batter's body twists, his shoulder level changes, although his hips and head stay level.

Hitting the ball
At this point, the batter has swung his arms around to the front and his shoulders are starting to straighten up.

Different angles

Don't just draw the front view of a figure, but instead explore the way a person looks from all angles – front, back, side, even upside down! Try drawing figures in different positions, too, from batting and dancing to sleeping.

Over the shoulder
Look at the angles the batter's body makes when he is leaning with all his weight on one foot.

HONORÉ DAUMIER *Family Scene c.1865*

In this drawing, Daumier managed to show the pride and tenderness that the parents feel for their young child. The quivering pen-and-ink line suits both the mood and the cheerful scruffiness of the family group. The artist has drawn each figure from a different angle, and given each of them their own particular character and expression.

Drawing faces

Drawing in proportion is something we learn gradually by looking closely. Young children tend to draw a person as a large head with tiny legs – they don't bother with the parts in between! Through close observation, you can learn to recognize the relationship between the features on people's faces and start to draw people who look more lifelike.

ARABELLA (aged 4)
Self-portrait 1994

SAM (aged 6)
Self-portrait 1994

SARAH CAWKWELL *Mending 1993*

Sarah Cawkwell uses delayed action photography to record herself doing everyday tasks, then makes large charcoal drawings from these photographs. Working from photographs can help you draw difficult subjects, such as the foreshortened head seen here.

Measure it out

Try drawing a picture from a photograph. Measure the position of the mouth, nose, eyes, and ears and make sure they are in proportion in your drawing.

Caricature

Grotesque figures, or caricatures, have a long history, and can even be seen in the margins of medieval manuscripts. John Tenniel, who illustrated *Alice in Wonderland*, was a great caricaturist. A caricature artist distorts features in order to emphasize certain characteristics of a person. Look out for caricatures of real people in newspapers and magazines. To be successful, the drawing must still look like the person it is caricaturing.

Drawing in the style of JOHN TENNIEL
Punch as Artist

Speed and energy

Sometimes you have only a moment to capture the dynamic energy of a moving or changing scene. To do this, you need bold, flowing strokes that show basic shapes, directions, and positions. The swiftly made marks will give a sense of urgency that can bring energy to your drawing. But to draw quickly you need to practice looking closely and controlling your strokes, as there won't be time for corrections.

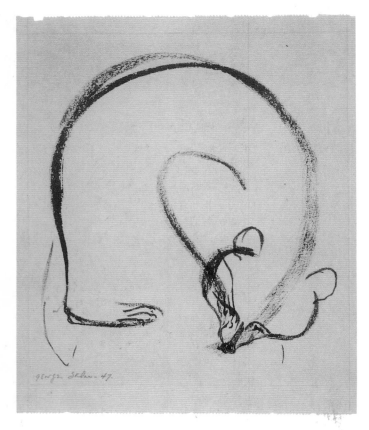

GEORGE SKLAR *Raccoon 1947*

With a great sweeping curve for the back and a few strokes for head and foot, the artist has swiftly captured the essential nature of this raccoon.

Fast drawing

Make quick sketches of people at the park, football field, playground, swimming pool, or beach. Try to capture movement without concerning yourself with details, such as people's faces or the patterns on their clothes.

Adding drama

Once you have made your lightning sketch, you can give drama to your drawing by adding a few heavier lines and some details.

Equipment for fast drawing

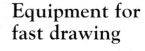

Graphite pencil

Soft pencil

Fine felt-tip pen

Charcoal

Pastel

BEN SHAHN *Out 1956*

Ben Shahn's simple drawings focus on dramatic moments in the lives of ordinary people. He drew with strong energetic lines, almost like a cartoonist. His pictures have the same strong characters and humor as a cartoon, too.

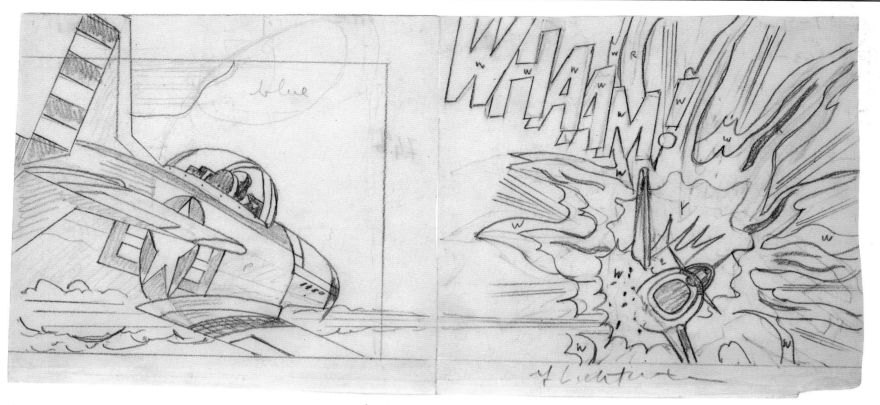

ROY LICHTENSTEIN *Drawing for Whaam! 1963*

Many of Lichtenstein's large paintings are based on comic-strip images. This is an early drawing for the painting *WHAAM!*, a bold design with bright, flat colors and strong, black outlines. He wanted to show dramatic subject matter in an unemotional and objective style, just as it might have been reported in the press.

Drawing energy

Antoine Gros was a 19th-century artist who enjoyed depicting dramatic scenes. The speed and immediacy of this brush drawing is used to express the violent energy of the rearing stallion and the horseman.

Energetic line

In the Lichtenstein drawing above, the lines show movement in two directions and suggest the deadly, mechanical action of the warplane. Compare this to the swirling brushstrokes of the horse's mane in the drawing of the horse and man, which capture something of the wildness of the animal. Each style relates directly to what the artist wanted to communicate in his picture. If you switched styles, the meaning of each picture would change.

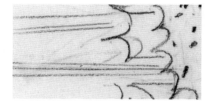

Mechanical movement
Look at the crisp lines of the rocket's path and the starburst pattern of the explosion.

Natural movement
The mark to the right of the mane shows the strong twist in the horse's neck muscles.

Drawing in the style of
ANTOINE GROS

BEN SHAHN *National Pastime 1956*

Look at the way the artist has bunched up the backstop figures and made the batter's limbs extra long. He has used a thick to thin line to suggest the swipe of the bat.

Drawing animals

The very first artists were prehistoric people who drew animals on rocks, perhaps as part of hunting rituals. Today, artists are still inspired by animal forms and features. Drawing an animal, whether it is a pet, a farm animal or a wild animal, will demand all your powers of observation and technique to capture the anatomy, surface textures, character, and movement. Start by drawing an animal when it is asleep, as animals have a habit of moving just when you don't want them to!

HENRI GAUDIER-BRZESKA *Eland 1912*

The French sculptor Gaudier-Brzeska loved drawing animals and birds. Using a few contour lines, he revealed the bony structure and gracefulness of this eland, a type of antelope.

Animal shapes

When you want to draw an animal, it can help to think about the basic shapes that fit into or make up the animal.

A solid body
Look for the angles of this massive body.

Look at the shapes that have been laid on top of this photograph of an elephant. Can you see that the elephant's frame is made up of rectangles and a triangle? Now make a simple drawing of your chosen animal, using shapes to help you.

REMBRANDT VAN RIJN *Elephant 1637*

The great Dutch artist Rembrandt made many drawings of animals, including this elephant that he saw at a circus. This crumbly black chalk sketch emphasizes the elephant's bulky roundness and the wrinkly texture of its skin. The people near the animal's head give us a sense of its huge size. Do you think the elephant looks friendly?

Animals in motion

It is not easy to draw moving animals, but it's worth giving it a try! Look at the photograph (right) of horses racing, and notice what happens to their legs. When you actually watch a horse running, everything moves so fast that you can't see exactly how the position of the legs changes. Before drawing pictures of running animals from memory, find photographs in books, magazines, or the sports pages of a newspaper, and work from those.

Choose a clear photograph, like this one by Robert Hallam, to work from.

Look closely at the shapes and shadows.

ALBRECHT DÜRER *Hare 1502*

The German artist Dürer drew this magnificent hare over 400 years ago. He looked closely at the shape of the head, ears, body, and legs and how they fitted together. Using various types of marks, he showed the textures and the way the light fell on the rippling waves of fur and velvety, upraised ears.

Feathers, skin, and fur

As well as studying an animal's shape, look closely at the pattern and texture of its feathers, fur, or skin. Think about the most appropriate drawing tools and marks to use for each surface.

Drawing birds

Not all feathers are the same. Look closely at the different textures and colors of the feathers on this male mandarin duck. You can draw birds with all sorts of different materials.

Brush lines show the general shape of a feather.

Charcoal can be slightly blended to form feathers.

Pencil lines capture the details and texture of a feather.

Snake skin can be shown using a thin watercolor wash over pen-drawn scales.

Draw your pet

One of the reasons why animals are popular subjects for drawing is that people love their pets and want to keep a record of them. Draw a picture of your own pet, perhaps in its favorite place. Spend time looking before you start. Study the shape of the animal's head and body, and the texture of its coat. Is its fur sleek or rough? What is the expression on its face?

Alice (aged 9) *My Cat 1994*

Dog hair can be drawn using close, wavy pen lines.

Wool is made using small swirls with a soft pencil.

Sketching ideas

Artists' sketchbooks are a treasure-house of ideas. In them, we discover first thoughts, observations, memories, and experimentation that may later emerge in finished works of art. It is useful to carry a small sketchbook at all times so that you can sketch the outline or capture the mood of something you see, or record an idea when it arises. At other times, you may use a larger sketchbook for detailed studies from life.

Fine charcoal

Thick charcoal

Soft pencil

Fine felt-tip pen

Sketching materials
When you plan to spend time sketching, take a variety of drawing materials with you.

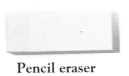

Pencil eraser

Pastel

Pencil sharpener

Getting ready
For close-up studies, try a sharpened pencil. For buildings, you may need to use a ruler. For landscapes, try a looser style using charcoal or pastel.

OSKAR KOKOSCHKA *Views of London: Tower Bridge 2 1967*

The Austrian Expressionist artist Kokoschka adopted London as his second home. He made thousands of sketches during his long life. He was over 80 when he filled his sketchbook with views of the Thames. In this drawing, notice how his few hastily drawn lines have captured the structure of this bridge, and how a squiggle of charcoal suggests the deep waters of the river beneath a small tugboat.

Sketching notes
Making sketches of things you see will help you look more closely at people and places. Take some notes to remind yourself of colors, light sources, weather, and other details.

Drawing surface
Use a sketchbook with a stiff back, or take something with you to lean on while you draw.

A place to sit
For sketching outdoors, find a place to sit that gives you a clear view of your subject. If you are sitting high up, looking down on the subject, you will get a different viewpoint from eye level. Pick a spot that is sheltered and check that you are not in anyone's way.

Odds and ends

Collect all sorts of things to give you ideas for patterns and shapes to use in later drawings. Arrange your collection carefully on the page and glue the items in place. Display bulky items on a shelf or keep them in a box.

Sketchbook collection

You can use your sketchbook for more than just drawing. Collect souvenirs from vacations and trips, and note down ideas. There is also an enormous variety of interesting things to find with unusual designs or colors, or images you want to remember. Look for bus and exhibition tickets, bank notes, even chocolate wrappers. You may be able to use your collection as inspiration for a completely new drawing.

Rough sketch
On the top page, the artist has made a very quick rough sketch of a house with a tree outside.

Color notes
In this more detailed, close-up sketch, the artist has written notes about color and other details he wants to remember for his finished drawing or painting.

Café scene
This sketch was drawn quickly in pencil to capture the activity of people in a café.

People and places

It is useful to develop different styles of sketching, as these two sketchbooks show. The style of a sketch depends on what you are drawing – it may be a quickly changing scene, or a building or landscape.

Greek church
This pastel sketch is more detailed, showing the colors and the effect of the light. It could be worked up into a painting later.

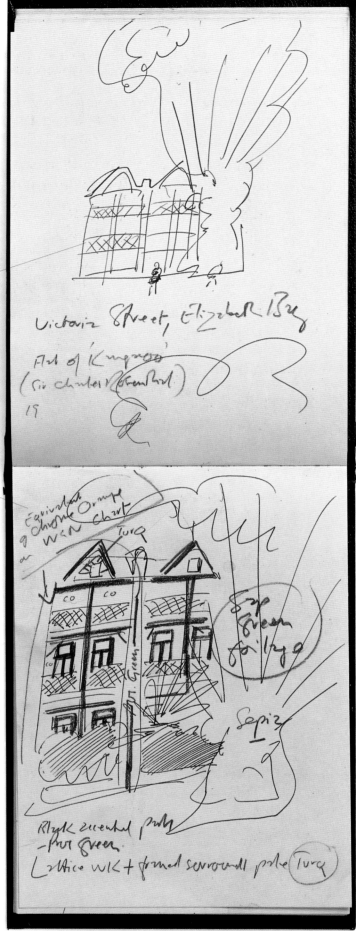

PAUL HOGARTH *Sketches of Sydney, Australia 1991*

These drawings are from Paul Hogarth's travel sketchbook. The sketches are very quick and rough but contain information that will help the artist to make a more detailed drawing or painting later on. Can you see the notes about where he was in the top sketch?

Imagination and storytelling

So far, we have been concentrating mainly on drawing what you see. But it's also important to use imagination in your drawings. You can make up scenes, create fantasy figures, tell stories in pictures or comic strips, illustrate poems or pieces of music – let your imagination run wild! Have fun playing with new ideas and creating your own unique pictures.

Looking for inspiration
Often your imaginative drawings will be inspired by things you see or hear around you. Looking at artists' works, reading books and comics, and listening to stories and songs can all inspire imaginative drawings.

Drawing in the style of
JOAN MIRÓ

VICTOR HUGO *The Octopus 1864–65*

This was one of a series of drawings completed after Hugo had written his popular novel *Toilers of the Sea*. He enjoyed experimenting with ink blots, using them as illustrations for his stories. Here, he has used a stain on the back of the paper as a background for his drawing.

Drawing atmosphere
Water-soluble pencils can be used like ordinary pencils, or brushed over with a wash. In an imaginative drawing, they can be used to create mysterious effects, such as strange, swirling mists.

The wave
Transform an ink blot doodle into a ship being tossed on the waves.

Strange animal
Add an outline to an ink blot to make a hippopotamus.

Doodle game

Scribbles, doodles, and blots often produce good results that were not planned. Try this simple game, played in pairs. Have a friend make a quick doodle or scribble. Now try to turn it into a picture by adding just a few simple details. Can you see two faces in this inky shape?

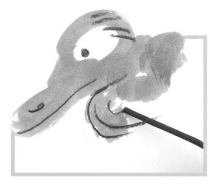

1 Brush watercolor or ink onto a piece of paper, making any abstract shape or pattern that you like.

2 Take a piece of charcoal and draw lines on top of the watercolor or ink to make a fantasy creature.

Storyboards

Storyboards are panels showing a sequence of drawings of the key moments in a story that is to be made into a film. They show the director, cameraman, and lighting engineer how the scene should look on screen. Each picture shows the right viewpoint, lighting, and positions for the actors.

TOM MORAHAN *Storyboard for the film* So Evil My Love *1948*

Drawn in pen and wash, this storyboard shows dramatic viewpoints and shadows, looking down on the street and up at the figures in the dome. Look at the effects of light and shade in the drawing. What sort of film do you think this is?

From storyboard to screen

This photographic frame from the film *So Evil My Love* shows a scene that the art director, Tom Morahan, had drawn in his storyboard (above). The stage set and the position of the actors in the photograph are almost exactly as he drew them in the storyboard.

Illustrating stories

In children's books, drawings of the characters and their adventures are an important part of the story. An illustrator has to work closely with the author to capture the mood of the story and come up with characters and scenes that look just right.

Comic-strip story

Draw your own story, either in episodes or in a single picture. Vary the shape and size of the frames and let characters break out of the borders.

EDWARD ARDIZZONE *The Little Bookroom 1955*

Edward Ardizzone's lively pen drawings are found in over 200 books. He drew small vignettes, using fine cross-hatching to create atmosphere.

Adapting your drawings

A drawing can be an end in itself, or it can be just one step in a process. Many artists use drawings to work out ideas and adjust their compositions before turning them into paintings, collages, models, murals, or sculptures. Here are some suggestions on how you might like to take your drawings a step further.

Pick one of your own drawings to enlarge.

Making your picture bigger

Artists use grids to make a small drawing larger. They may want to transfer their picture from a small sheet of paper to a large canvas or wall. This process is called "squaring up" because the original drawing is enlarged, section by section, or square by square. Try this enlarging technique to make a small drawing, like the one above, into a larger drawing or painting.

SIR STANLEY SPENCER *Shipbuilding on the Clyde* 1940

Commissioned to paint a mural of Glasgow shipbuilding during World War II, the English artist Stanley Spencer first made many detailed drawings. Look how he squared up this drawing so that he could enlarge it.

Square grid of larger size

1 Using a set square, draw a grid of squares on your drawing. Draw another grid of larger squares onto plain paper.

Detail of finished mural
Spencer used his drawings as a reference for this huge mural, finished in 1946.

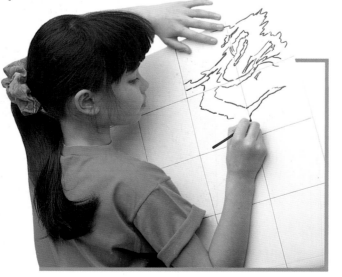

2 Follow the lines of your first drawing, filling in each square until you have an enlarged version. Use this method to make your drawing as big as you like.

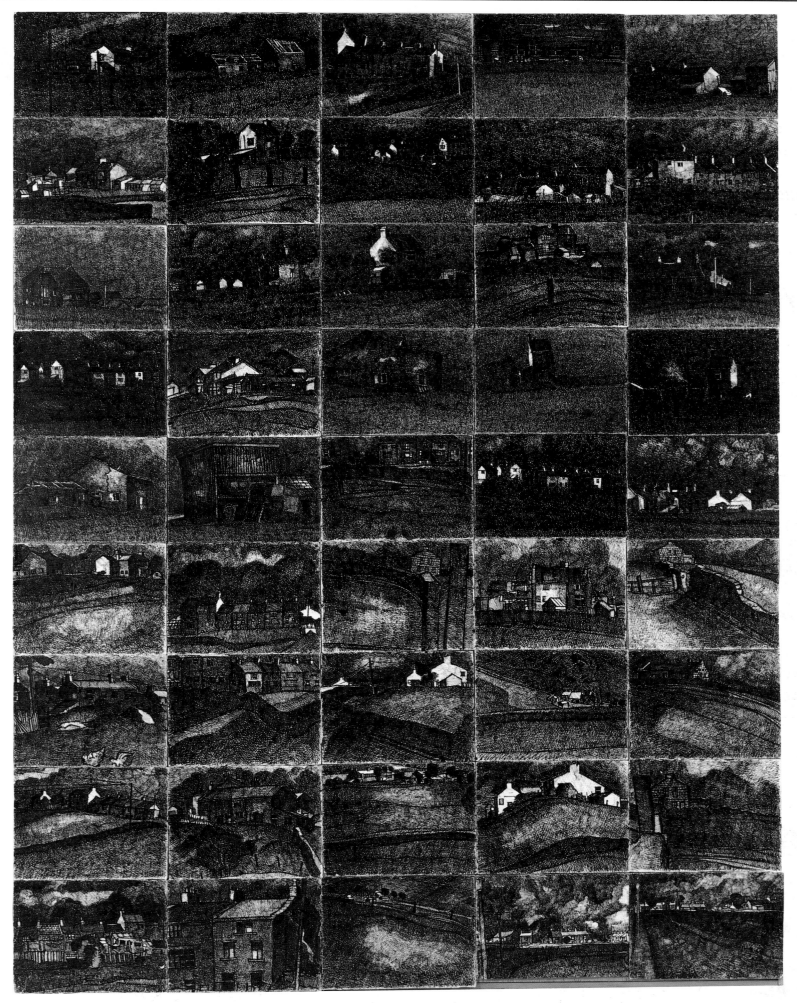

JOHN VIRTUE *Landscape No. 6 1978–81*

John Virtue makes richly dark drawings, often only postcard size, around the village in England where he lives. Over a period of days or weeks, he builds up different views of the same area and puts these together to form a large patchwork grid of black and white images.

Drawing collage
Make lots of drawings on the same size sheets of paper, then join them together to create a bigger picture.

About the artists

Edward Ardizzone (1900–1979, British) was a popular illustrator of children's books, some of which he wrote himself. During World War II, he traveled with the soldiers, recording their lives.

Léon Bonvin (1834–1866, French) grew up poor. Although both he and his brother François learned painting at a free school in Paris, Léon was mainly self-taught. He could not make a living as a painter and so opened a restaurant in Plaisance, which artists of the area went to. In 1866 he hanged himself in the woods at Meudon.

Sonia Boyce (born 1962, British) is a leading young artist who has been widely exhibited. Much of her work explores personal themes.

Mary Cassatt (1845–1926, American) settled in Paris in 1868, where she exhibited her work with the Impressionists. She was a friend of Berthe Morisot and Manet. Her work shows a woman's views of Parisian life.

Sarah Cawkwell (born 1950, British) uses her drawing to focus on the work of women at home, which is often ignored by other artists.

John Constable (1776–1837, British) was one of the leading landscape artists of his day. His landscape paintings of the English countryside were composed in his studio, based on drawings and color sketches made outdoors.

Honoré Daumier (1808–1879, French) worked as a cartoonist and satirical illustrator. His drawings of everyday life capture the desperate poverty of many people in France at the time.

Edgar Degas (1834–1917, French) was most famous for his drawings of dancers and other female models. He came from a rich family, so he did not have to make money from his art. This meant that he could experiment with his work more than less fortunate artists of his time.

Raoul Dufy (1877–1953, French) became famous for bright, breezy subjects such as seaside esplanades and horse races. As well as painting and drawing, he also designed ceramics and textiles. Rapid strokes and simple, decorative shapes give his work a fresh energy.

Albrecht Dürer (1471–1528, German) was the son of a goldsmith, and one of the finest draftsmen in the history of art. He is most famous for highly detailed woodcut prints and engravings, and his drawings and paintings show the same technical brilliance.

Maurits Corneille Escher (1898–1972, Dutch) created strange, detailed prints that seem very realistic at first glance. When they are looked at more closely, they suddenly turn into impossible visual puzzles that are very difficult to untangle.

Henri Gaudier-Brzeska (1891–1915, French) was an outstanding sculptor who lived in London for the last four years of his short life before he was killed in World War I at the age of 24. He captured the energy and grace of various animals in a series of drawings made at the London Zoo.

Anthony Green RA (born 1939, British) paints detailed domestic scenes that are often amusing. He plays with ideas of perspective in his work, especially by using strangely shaped canvases.

Brian Grimwood (born 1948, British) is an illustrator whose work can be seen in publications around the world. He usually works in pen and ink or watercolor.

Hans Hofmann (1880–1966, German, became a US citizen) founded his own school of art in New York in the 1930s. He pioneered the technique of pouring and dribbling paint in abstract patterns onto a canvas, which was made famous by the American artist Jackson Pollock.

Paul Hogarth RA (born 1917, British) is best known for his pictures of faraway and exotic places. He has illustrated books by many famous writers, as well as producing his own books.

Victor Hugo (1802–1885, French) was a writer, famous for books such as *Les Misérables*, who sometimes illustrated his own books.

Jean Auguste Dominique Ingres (1780–1867, French) was the son of an artist. His father noticed his son's amazing talent at an early age and sent him away to study art when he was 11. Ingres lived in Italy for many years and became famous as a portrait artist. He believed that drawing skills were the basis of truly great art.

Zdenka Kabátová-Táborská (born 1933, Czech) uses woodcut techniques for her work. She has produced illustrations for many books, especially fairy tales and other books for children. She lives and works in Prague in the Czech Republic.

Ernst Ludwig Kirchner (1880–1938, German) was a painter, sculptor, and printmaker. He was a leading member of the Brücke group of German Expressionists.

Paul Klee (1879–1940, Swiss) experimented with patterns of lines and shapes, and created fantasy works with a very poetic quality. He described his work as "taking a line for a walk."

Oskar Kokoschka (1886–1980, Austrian) spent most of his life in Germany, where he became a major figure in early 20th-century art. He was a teacher at the famous Bauhaus. His work explores the fears and fantasies of modern life.

Fernand Léger (1881–1955, French) celebrated modern life using bright, flat colors and strong black outlines. His figures were inspired by machinery and city architecture.

Leonardo da Vinci (1452–1519, Italian) was famous not just as an artist and sculptor, but also as a scientist, musician, and engineer. His fascinating sketchbooks are full of notes and drawings, which combine all these interests.

Roy Lichtenstein (born 1923, American) is well known for his paintings of huge comic-strip frames. The dots and lines that make up a printed picture are greatly magnified in his work.

Henry Moore (1898–1986, British) was a major sculptor of the 20th century. His sculptures of the human body were based on natural forms, such as pebbles, bones, and shells. He also produced a huge number of drawings, including sketches that he later turned into sculptures.

Giorgio Morandi (1890–1964, Italian) lived in his home country all his life. He painted mainly still lifes, especially arrangements of bottles. His work reflects a quiet, thoughtful approach to life.

Pablo Picasso (1881–1973, Spanish) lived and worked in France. With another artist, Georges Braque, he developed a new approach to art called Cubism, which split subjects up into geometrical planes, showing them from several different angles at the same time. Picasso was one of the most influential artists of the 20th century.

Rembrandt van Rijn (1606–1669, Dutch) achieved success as a portrait painter. His self-portraits, painted throughout his life, record every stage of his career. He also made many paintings of his wife, Saskia, and of biblical subjects.

Nagasawa Rosetsu (1754–1799, Japanese) was a master of free, rapid brushwork. He was a larger than life character whose pictures are bold and expressive. Much of his work features animals.

Sir Peter Paul Rubens (1577–1640, Flemish) was Court Painter in Italy and the Netherlands. He produced large compositions on a variety of subjects, but even in a simple drawing, he shows light and form in a way that is full of life.

Ben Shahn (1898–1969, Lithuanian, became a US citizen) came from a family of carpenters, wood carvers, and potters, which gave him his strong interest in craft work. Many of his pictures deal with social and political subjects.

George Sklar (1905–1968, American) was born in Philadelphia, where he also studied and later taught. A sculptor, designer, and painter who specialized in animal subjects, he was a prize-winning exhibitor at the Ecole des Beaux-Arts in Paris in 1932.

Sir Stanley Spencer (1891–1959, British) spent most of his life in an English village called Cookham, where he was born. Some of his most famous works are scenes from life in Cookham as the setting for events from the Bible.

Francis Unwin (1885–1925, British) was a painter and etcher who specialized in landscapes and architectural images.

Vincent van Gogh (1853–1890, Dutch) was born in the Netherlands, but settled in Paris in the 1880s. His paintings and drawings, on all kinds of subjects, are direct and simple, but also powerful and passionate.

John Virtue (born 1947, British) lived in the British countryside for many years. He was inspired by the local landscape and has created large pieces made up of many individual pen-and-ink drawings.

Index

Acknowledgments

PICTURE CREDITS
Every effort has been made to trace the copyright holders and we apologize for any unintentional omissions. We would be pleased to insert the appropriate acknowledgment in any subsequent edition of this publication.

Key:
t: top b: bottom l: left r: right c: center

© Addison Gallery of American Art, Phillips Academy, Andover, Massachusetts. All rights reserved. Hans Hofmann, *Color Intervals at Provincetown*, 1943, ink and crayon on wove paper, 11x14in., 1948.13. **18b**; © Edward Ardizzone, from *The Glass Peacock (The Little Bookroom)* by Eleanor Farjeon, permission granted by the author **41br**; photographs ©1994, The Art Institute of Chicago. All rights reserved. Jean-Auguste-Dominique Ingres, French, 1780-1867, *Charles Francois Mallet, Civil Engineer*, graphite, on cream wove paper, 1809, 26.8x21.1cm, Charles Deering Collection, 1938.166. **30br**/Edgar Degas, French, 1834-1917, *Three Studies of a Dancer in Fourth Position*, charcoal and pastel with stumping, with touches of brush and black wash on grayish-tan laid paper with blue fibers (discolored from pinkish-blue), c.1879/80, 48x61.5cm, Bequest of Adele R.Levy,

1962-703 **32tr**/Honore Daumier, French, 1808-1879, *Family Scene*, pen and black ink, and brush and gray wash, on ivory wove paper (discolored to cream), c.1867-70, 21.6x20.5cm, Helen Regenstein Collection, 1965.633 **32br**; Collection Arts Council of Great Britain, South Bank Centre, London **43**; BFI Stills, Posters & Designs/© MCA Universal **41tr,cl**; Bibliotheque Nationale/Michele Jacqinet **40tr**; Biblioteca Reale, Torino **16tr**; British Museum **8br, 36cr**; Sarah Cawkwell **33t**; © 1994 M.C. Escher/Cordon Art- Baarn- Holland. All rights reserved **22bl**; Gimpel Fils Gallery **23tr**; Graphische Sammlung Albertina, Vienna **37t**; Anthony Green/Piccadilly Gallery, London **29t**; Brian Grimwood **21br**; Paul Hogarth/Folio **39r**; Imperial War Museum, London, Stanley Spencer, *Shipbuilding on the Clyde*, **42cl,bl**; The Independent/Robert Hallam **36bc**; Zdenka Kabátová-Táborská, *Evening of Fairytales*, J.Hadislav, Albatross, Prague 1992 **24cl**; Fernand Leger, *The Birthday*, 1950, © DACS 1994 **FC, 20bl**; Okamoto Masanori, Wakayama **26br**; Musée d'Art Moderne de la Communaute Urbaine de Lille, Villeneuve d' Ascq. Donation Genevieve et Jean Masurel, Pablo Picasso, *Head of a Man*, 1912 © DACS 1994 **9cr**; The Nelson-Atkins Museum of Art, Kansas City, Missouri (Purchase: Acquired through the generosity of an anonymous donor) F77-33. Drawing- Pastel- American (active in France) Mary Cassatt (1845-1926) *At the Theater (Woman in a*

Loge), ca.1879. Pastel on paper 21-13/16"x18-1/8"(55.4x46.1cm) **19t**; Philadelphia Museum of Art: Given by Miss Edith B. Thompson, George Sklar, *Racoon*, 1947 **34cl**; © Photo R.M.N., Léon Bonvin, *Still Life*, **10br**; Ben Shahn, *National Pastime*, and *"Out,"* 1956 © Estate of Ben Shahn/DACS, London/VAGA, New York 1994 **34-5b**; Stadelsches Kunstinstitut, Frankfurt a.M. Photo: Ursula Edelmann, Frankfurt a.M. **15tr**; Tate Gallery, London **17, 25cl, 36tr**/Raoul Dufy, *Open Window at Saint Jeannet* c.1926-7 © DACS 1994. **27tr**/Oskar Kokoschka, *Tower Bridge*, 1967 © DACS 1994 **38bl**; Giorgio Morandi, *Still Life* © DACS 1994 **28bl**/Roy Lichtenstein, *Whaam*, 1963 © Roy Lichtenstein/DACS 1994 **35t,c**; Victoria and Albert Museum **16bc**; Collection Vincent Van Gogh Foundation/Van Gogh Museum, Amsterdam **14c**; Grahame L.Walsh, Takarakka Rock Art Research Center **8tr**.

Dorling Kindersley would like to thank Gill Mitra, the teachers and pupils of Rhodes Avenue Primary School, London; Claire Archer for design help; Bev Brennan for drawings on pages 16, 26/27, 30, and 37; Jane Gifford for the drawings on page 22; Ann Kay for "About the Artists" on page 44; Lynn Bresler for the index; Jerry Young for photographs on pages 39(r) and 43.

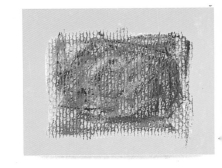